SafetyInformed.org's

Emergency Plan

Workbook

5th Edition

A
SafetyInformed.org
Publication

SafetyInformed.org's Emergency Plan Workbook
Copyright © 2015 by *SafetyInformed, LLC.*

ISBN: 978-1507863244

Follow Us:
Facebook: http://facebook.com/safetyinformed
Twitter: http://twitter.com/safetyinformed
Google+: http://google.com/+SafetyinformedUniversity

Visit our blog for more useful articles and tidbits on this topic:
http://safetyinformed.org/blog

Table of Contents

How to Use This Workbook

This workbook is a supplement to our free online *Emergency Basics Course*. It consists of five modules with accompanying worksheets that you'll need to create your Emergency Plan. There are links to important resources for gathering information, supplies, etc. and detailed instructions on how to set up Reverse 911 alerts in your area using our national ZIP code search tool.

If you purchased this publication as a physical book or through an eBook reader, we want to *thank you for supporting us*! Your purchase helps us keep our Reverse 911 search service up-to-date and continue to create important educational materials.

Download the free PDF version of this workbook for printer-friendly worksheets:

http://safetyinformed.org/download/emergency-plan-workbook (PDF)

Help us spread Reverse 911 in your community.

Please share the free PDF version of this book or order additional copies as gifts for your friends, neighbors and coworkers through our web site:

To share with friends: http://safetyinformed.org/share

You can support us by ordering copies of this book through Amazon.com: http://safetyinformed.org/order/epw

Module 1:
Setting Up Emergency Notifications

Disasters can affect any part of the United States at any time of the year, swiftly and without warning. Most people don't think of what to do in the event of a natural disaster or community emergency until it is too late; then they suddenly realize how unprepared they are for the massive changes it can make in their lives. On top of that, local officials can be overwhelmed and emergency response personnel may not be able to reach everyone who needs help right away. Each type of disaster requires clean up and recovery and the period after a disaster is often very difficult for families and can be as devastating as the disaster itself. Families that are prepared ahead of time can reduce the fear, confusion and losses that come with disaster. They can be ready to evacuate their homes, know what to expect in public shelters and how to provide basic first aid.

The key to successfully managing any emergency is being prepared ahead of time but even more critical is being informed that an emergency is headed your way. Whether it's a tornado, fire, flood or broken gas line, just having even a few minutes' notice can make the difference between life and death.

If an emergency or natural disaster occurred in your community, how would you know when to evacuate or avoid affected areas? That's where Reverse 911 comes in.

Unlike traditional Emergency Notification Systems that rely on a phone line at your home address or being near a cell tower within affected areas, if you register Reverse 911 services will send the most precise warnings and instructions you can receive in the event of danger to life or property no matter where you are.

During and after common emergencies such as: wildfire, flood, severe weather, industrial accidents, and police action, local emergency officials send text and email alerts to residents of an affected area with precise warnings and instructions. In most situations, Reverse 911 alerts can be sent 20 minutes before traditional news and social media even notice an emergency event from afar. In many cases, Reverse 911 has alerted residents of an affected area hours before a news crew reports it. It just depends on the scale of the event and how "newsworthy" it is.

The point is that even if a news reports or buzz on social media begins to spread during an emergency, you're not likely to get the exact information you need for your area. Reverse 911 alerts come directly from emergency responders that are managing the event.

So how do you find your local Reverse 911 system?

To receive Reverse 911 notifications, register your mobile number and physical address with your community Emergency Response Center.

SafetyInformed has provided you with the tool you need to freely register with your local Reverse 911 system. And while Reverse 911 varies from community to community, we have incorporated into our search tool the pathway to access your local emergency alerts; for you and the other important members of your family by simply searching for them by ZIP code.

This will only take a few minutes and when you are done you will have the peace of mind that you are on the list of people to notify in case of an emergency in your area.

Find Your Reverse 911 System with our ZIP code search:

If you downloaded this book from safetyinformed.org then login to your account and search by going here: http://safetyinformed.org/login

If you purchased or were given this book from another web site, then visit our web site and click "Set Up Reverse 911" on the page here: http://safetyinformed.org

Then watch the "Show me How" video to learn how to register every mobile phone in your family so that you can be alerted of emergencies affecting other family members in different locations—from across town to across the country.

This first step is critical to the survival of your family in an emergency!

Stay Informed ...

Our team is dedicated to providing you with the tips, tools, and the important information you need to prepare your family for any emergency through our blog posts. To get regular access to these resources be sure to follow us on Facebook, Twitter, or Google+:

Facebook: http://facebook.com/safetyinformed
Twitter: http://twitter.com/safetyinformed
Google+: http://google.com/+SafetyinformedUniversity

Help us spread Reverse 911 in your community.

Please share the free PDF version of this book or order additional copies as gifts for your friends, neighbors and coworkers through our web site:

To share with friends: http://safetyinformed.org/share

You can support us by ordering copies of this book through Amazon.com: http://safetyinformed.org/order/epw

Module 2:
Your Emergency Plan

While disasters come in many varieties, there are elements of preparedness that apply in all cases, and the beginning of the preparation process is being informed of what you can do to get your family ready. We will take you through exactly what you need to do to get your home and your family ready to respond to emergencies before they happen. And what we share doesn't involve the purchase of a lot of special equipment and supplies. The majority of what you need to go along with becoming properly informed and prepared you will already find in your home or with a quick trip to the store.

It's true that planning for survival can entail a great amount of detail and take a lot of time. On the other hand, the greater part of your planning really just involves common sense. But many families haven't taken the time necessary to think through the preparation process to discover the simple steps they need to take. With just a few minutes each day you can get your home organized and begin the process of preparing everyone to make the quick response necessary to get out of harm's way the moment you receive an emergency alert through Reverse 911.

We know that it's difficult for most of us to set aside the time to plan ahead for a crisis or disaster, so our team has developed an easy way to help you develop your family's personal emergency plan with this workbook. It's designed to serve as a simple guide for your entire family to safely come through an emergency as quickly and efficiently as possible. If you haven't already, download and print out the PDF version of this book so you can fill out the included emergency planning worksheets.

Download the *Emergency Plan Workbook* as a PDF here:
http://safetyinformed.org/download/emergency-plan-workbook

1. Do Your Homework...

Find out what natural disasters could happen in your area by contacting your local Emergency Management Service (EMS). They are prepared to tell you which disasters are possible where you live and how they might affect your family. You can obtain information on how to prepare and respond to each potential disaster. They will point out things that we don't often think about such as caring for you animals. Pets are frequently not allowed inside shelters because of health regulations so you need to have an alternative plan in place.

> *Tip:* To find your local emergency management agency simply Google "<your-county-name or city-name> emergency management."

Your local emergency management agency most likely has a dedicated web site and social media presence to find all the information you need about the most common emergencies and natural disasters in your area. In more rural areas, dedicated emergency management resources may not be available, so contact the nearest one possible to gather this information.

> To help with information gathering and family discussion, all the known natural disasters can be found, along with what to do before, during and after, in our *Disaster Preparedness Library* free at:
> http://safetyinformed.org/education/hazard

2. Create a Family Emergency Plan...

Discuss with your family the need to prepare for and the types of disasters that are most likely to occur in your area and how the family is going to respond in each case. For example, explain the danger of fire, severe weather (tornadoes, hurricanes) and floods to your children and then develop a plan for them to share in the responsibilities so you can work together as a team. Establish meeting places inside and outside your home, as well as outside the neighborhood and make sure everyone knows when and how to contact each other if separated. An important step is to decide on the best escape routes from your home and identifying two ways out of each room. You should also establish a family contact that is out-of-town; a friend or relative. Call this person after the disaster to let them know where you are and if you are okay. Make sure everyone knows the contact's phone number. Learn what to do if you are advised to evacuate.

3. Make a Checklist and Periodically Update it...

Post emergency telephone numbers by phones (fire, police, ambulance, etc.) and teach your children how and when to call 911 or your local EMS number for help. Identify safe places in your home to go for each type of disaster. Check to be sure you have adequate insurance coverage.

Each family member should know how to turn off the water, gas, and electricity at the main valves or switches. Teach each family member how to use a fire extinguisher (ABC type) and have a central place to keep it and be sure that it's checked every six months. Install smoke detectors on each level of your home, especially near bedrooms, and check the batteries twice a year. Stock emergency supplies and assemble a disaster supply kit. Utilize the Red Cross resources to learn basic first aid and make sure that each family member knows CPR, how to help someone who is choking, and first aid for severe bleeding and shock.

At the end of this module are links to American Red Cross Resources that range from taking a First-Aid course in your area, online courses and references apps you can load on your smartphone. Taking a local first-aid course is the best option and for a nominal fee you'll get the next best thing to firsthand experience.

4. Practice and Maintain Your Plan...

Test your children's knowledge of the family plan every six months so they will remember what to do. It's also a good idea to conduct fire and emergency evacuation drills at the same time and as part of your drill you should test your smoke detectors and change the batteries. It's also a good idea, in conjunction with your preparedness plan, to work with your neighbors to plan how the neighborhood could work together after a disaster until help arrives. Know their special skills (medical, technical) and consider how to help those who have special needs.

Now, as you read through the first two sections and fill out the information, take the time to add personal notes that apply specifically to you and your family. These first two sections focus on ensuring that you are alerted to any emergency and where and how your family is to assemble to stay together as a unit. In addition, this is the place to cover the responsibilities of each member of the family.

Each section builds together to provide you with a well thought out plan for immediate execution by everyone in your family. Be sure that you keep your plan in a safe place where each member of the family can quickly access it.

Without planning, uncertainty and chaos will quickly rule the day, but with proper preparation they can be overcome by knowledge. Your family will be prepared to respond quickly, safely, and efficiently. Just remember that your emergency plan is a living document and you need to review and update it regularly so that when it's needed there will be no glitches in carrying it out.

Worksheet

Fill out *Worksheet: Emergency Plan*

Supplemental Materials

First-Aid Kits We Recommend:
http://safetyinformed.org/blog/affordable-first-aid-kits

Planning for Family Members with Access and Functional Needs:
http://safetyinformed.org/blog/family-members-with-access-and-functional-needs

American Red Cross First-Aid Training:
http://www.redcross.org/take-a-class

American Red Cross Online Family First-Aid Course:
http://www.redcross.org/take-a-class/course-dowbt000000000010278

American Red Cross First-Aid Smartphone Apps:
http://www.redcross.org/prepare/mobile-apps
http://www.redcross.org/mobile-apps/first-aid-app
http://www.redcross.org/mobile-apps/pet-first-aid-app

Help us spread Reverse 911 in your community.

Please share the free PDF version of this book or order additional copies as gifts for your friends, neighbors and coworkers through our web site:

To share with friends: http://safetyinformed.org/share

You can support us by ordering copies of this book through Amazon.com:
http://safetyinformed.org/order/epw

Module 3:
If We Need to Evacuate

Let's take a look at some of the issues you need to consider in planning for the event that you are forced to evacuate your home. At the end of this module we have provided a worksheet for you to record important information concerning things like who is evacuating with you and your family, what are your pre-planned escape routes, what is your primary and secondary transportation, what do you need to take with you, where are you going, etc.

Evacuations during a disaster are a common event and will vary by location and type of disaster. In light of that, one of the first steps you need to take is to become familiar with the current evacuation plans established by your local Emergency Management Service (EMS) or civil defense office. The amount of time you will have to evacuate depends on the disaster. Some disasters, such as hurricanes, may allow several days to prepare but hazardous materials accidents may only allow moments to leave. This means that advance preparation is essential since there may not be time to collect the basic necessities, and since some evacuations can last for several days you may be responsible for part or all of your own food, clothing, and other supplies.

Preparing for Evacuation

Any evacuation is stressful on a family so your advance planning is critical in making your evacuation easier and safer. Here are some examples of things you need to consider in preparing for an evacuation:

- Review possible evacuation procedures with your family and ask a friend or relative outside your area to be the check-in contact so that everyone in the family can call that person to say they are safe.

- Find out where children will be sent if they are in school when an evacuation is announced and how you will pick them up.

- Plan where you would go if you had to evacuate. Consider the homes of relatives or friends who live nearby, but outside the area of potential disaster.

- Have your family disaster supply kit and plan ready (detailed plans for building a family disaster supply kit can be found in the Supplemental Materials section at the end of this module)

- Contact your local emergency management office for community evacuation plans and identify and locate reception and shelter areas.

- Keep plenty of fuel in your car's gas tank at all times because during emergencies filling stations may be closed. Never store extra fuel in the garage.

- If you do not have a car or other vehicle, make transportation arrangements with friends, neighbors, or check with your local emergency management office for public services.

- Know where and how to shut off electricity, gas, and water at main switches and valves. Make sure you have the tools you need; usually pipe or adjustable wrenches.

Evacuating

When you are told to evacuate there are four important steps you need to take:

1. If there is time, secure your house by unplugging all of your appliances; especially all computers. In a flood hazard area be sure you store any propane tanks or secure them safely to the structure. Turn off the main water valve and take any actions needed to prevent damage to water pipes in freezing weather. Be sure to securely close and lock all doors, windows, and your garage (from the inside).

2. Follow the recommended evacuation routes you outlined ahead of time, but be aware of alternate routes as may be established by local authorities. *Do not take shortcuts, they may be blocked.*

3. Listen to the radio for emergency shelter information.

4. Be sure that you have your family disaster supply kit that contains any important medications.

There is also a planning element attached to returning home after the all clear has been given. Here are a few things to consider when developing your *Emergency Plan:*

Returning Home After the Disaster

- First and foremost… do not return home until the local authorities have authorized access. There may be leaking gas or other flammable materials present, and at your home only use battery-operated flashlights if you suspect a gas leak.

- If you smell leaking gas, turn off the main gas valve at the meter and open the windows if you can do so safely, and then leave the house immediately and notify the gas company or the fire department. Do not reenter the house until an authorized person tells you it is safe to do so.

- Notify the power company or fire department if you see any fallen or damaged electrical wires and stay clear.

- If any of your appliances are wet, turn off the main electrical power switch in your home before you unplug them. Be sure to dry out appliances, wall switches, and sockets before you use them in again. If you are in doubt at all about your electric, gas, or water services, call your utility companies for assistance.

- Check food and water supplies for contamination and spoilage before using them… if in doubt—throw it out.

And most importantly, after the emergency is over and your family is regrouped and safe, telephone your family and friends to tell them you are okay. It is so easy in the heat of the emergency to forget that there are those who are concerned about your safety.

Worksheet

Fill out *Worksheet: If We Need to Evacuate*

Supplemental Materials

Ready.gov guide on building an emergency supply kit:
http://www.ready.gov/build-a-kit

Affordable Evacuation Kits:
http://safetyinformed.org/blog/affordable-evacuation-kits-and-bug-out-bags

Affordable Emergency Supplies for Sheltering In-Place:
http://safetyinformed.org/blog/affordable-emergency-supplies

American Red Cross Shelter App:
http://www.redcross.org/mobile-apps/shelter-finder-app

Help us spread Reverse 911 in your community.

Please share the free PDF version of this book or order additional copies as gifts for your friends, neighbors and coworkers through our web site:

To share with friends: http://safetyinformed.org/share

You can support us by ordering copies of this book through Amazon.com: http://safetyinformed.org/order/epw

Module 4:
Emergency Communication Plan

Once you have registered with your local Reverse 911 System, you will be notified of any local emergencies affecting your area. But in addition, it's the wise household that keeps fully informed by monitoring other warning systems like those provided by the Emergency Alert System (EAS).

EAS is a national public warning system that requires broadcasters, cable television systems, wireless cable systems, and satellite radio and television broadcasters to provide the communications capability to the President to address the American public during a national emergency. EAS is also used by state and local authorities to deliver important emergency information, such as AMBER alerts and weather information targeted to specific areas.

The federal government, through the National Oceanic and Atmospheric Administration (NOAA), provides several emergency services that you can access, like the National Weather Service, the National Hurricane Service, the Ocean Prediction Center, Marine Forecasts and Aviation Weather. They all provide access to information directly related to your location. You can access these services on the Internet or, as in the case of sudden violent weather you can monitor the National Weather Service. And the best way to do that is with a weather radio.

Phone, internet and cell services may not be working, have a radio on hand. These inexpensive radios are readily available and will automatically activate with a voice message from the National Weather Service, day or night, to inform you of severe conditions in your area. Often times you will receive critical information at the same time it is received by your local Reverse 911 system. But communication from the outside is just the first step. You can find our regularly updated list of affordable emergency radios here: http://safetyinformed.org/blog/emergency-radios

In this module we cover an introduction to establishing the most important family lifeline… your Emergency Communication Plan. It doesn't matter whether the members of your family are across the country or just on the other side of town. You need to know if they are in danger so that you can contact them and initiate the survival plan we've helped you establish. You need to know that if they are facing imminent danger that you will be notified and that you have a plan to quickly get in contact with them.

Having a way to communicate with your family in times of an emergency is vital and making an emergency communication plan prior to a disaster is the only way to ensure everyone in your family knows how to keep in touch. A solid plan is the key to safely reuniting with your family.

Your plan will ensure that your family members are going to know where to find you if you are at work and a disaster strikes your building? Separation is particularly likely during the day when adults are at work and children are at school so you need to know how to reunite with your loved ones. If they are at home and something happens in the neighborhood and it has to be evacuated or there is a power outage you need to make sure where they are? Having a plan in place allows everyone to know where to meet and if they are unable to reach the planned location, they will know who to contact. Here are some things to consider before you begin filling out the Emergency Communication Plan worksheet:

Where to Meet

Your plan needs to clearly outline how your family will stay in contact if you get separated and cell service is not working. The first step to take is to identify two places away from your home where you will meet.

1. **In your neighborhood** – choose a place that is a safe distance from your home, such as under a tree or at a neighbor's house in case the emergency or disaster is at your house.

2. **Outside of your neighborhood** – choose a place such as a school playground, church or local park in case it's not possible to get to your home or neighborhood.

If you are prevented from getting to either location you need to have a designated person who can pick up your children at school or daycare, attend to any pets, and/or care for any elderly members of the family (at home or in facilities). This needs to be something that is done automatically if you are prevented from showing up at the prearranged location. Be sure the school or daycare staff has the name of that person on file.

How to Stay in Touch

Choose someone local for your family members to call as well as a long distance contact. An out-of-town contact may be in a better position to communicate with separated family members. Long distance calls may still go through when local phone service isn't working. If you are using your cell phone, the preferred method during a disaster is texting because it takes up less bandwidth.

1. *Pick an out-of-town contact*; a friend or relative who will be family's primary make contact with.

2. *Pick another out-of-town contact*; a friend or relative who will be your household's alternative contact.

3. Ensure that everyone in the family knows their names, addresses, and home and cell phone numbers; it's preferable to have them also carry that information with them.

In the event that communication systems prevent you from reaching your family, the Red Cross does offer an alternative. As soon as they get a shelter site set up, they can help you register on The American Red Cross Safe and Well website (see Worksheet). It is a central location for people in disaster areas in the United States to register their current status. That way, anyone in your family can check on you and see how you are doing. It really relieves stress for people who need updates on how their families are doing when reaching them by phone is impossible.

It's also a good idea to clearly identify and store the emergency numbers in every cell phone and post them beside your home phone. In addition, you should store the number of a person to contact in each member's cell phone under ICE (In Case of

Emergency) so authorities will know who to call in an emergency should you be unable to do so.

Implement the Plan

Having an emergency communication plan is great, but it won't do you any good if you don't put it all in place. Take the time to practice your plan with your family. That means actually going to the places you have designated as meeting places. Your family members, especially children, need to see those places. You have to implement the plan if it is going to work and to do that effectively everyone needs to be totally familiar with it.

Worksheet and Supplemental Materials
Worksheet: Emergency Communication Plan

Affordable Emergency Radios:
http://safetyinformed.org/blog/emergency-radios

American Red Cross Safe and Well Site:
http://www.redcross.org/find-help/contact-family/register-safe-listing

Recovering From a Natural Disaster:
http://safetyinformed.org/blog/recovering-from-a-natural-disaster/

Help us spread Reverse 911 in your community.

Please share the free PDF version of this book or order additional copies as gifts for your friends, neighbors and coworkers through our web site:

To share with friends: http://safetyinformed.org/share

You can support us by ordering copies of this book through Amazon.com:
http://safetyinformed.org/order/epw

Module 5:
Vital information Card

In the first four modules we highlighted how to get started, how to set up emergency notifications, what to do if you need to evacuate, and how to develop an emergency communication plan. In this module we want to look at the importance of developing a *Vital Information Card* for each member of your family.

In Module 4 we considered the fact that your family may not be together when disaster strikes, so you looked at planning how you will contact one another. As part of your Vital Information Card, you should complete a contact card for each family member. Have everyone keep their cards handy in a wallet, purse, backpack, etc. You may want to send one to school with each child to keep on file. The example is on suggestion from FEMA. And in today's "connected" world it is a good idea to put all of this information into each member's Smart Phone contact database using the same contact title (such as)—*Family Communication Plan.*

But this *Vital Information Card* contains only a part of the information you need to have available in case of an emergency. As you will see in the workbook, you should also keep a current record of each family member's electronic information in order to provide multiple channels for communication. That list should also contain the important contact information for your doctors, attorney, insurance agent, and any other professional you may need to communicate with. And with respect to medical issues, each family member's card should include any information concerning specific medical conditions, medicines (name and dosage), and the name and contact information of the attending physician. The same would apply to any elderly or disabled members of your family with special needs that require attention.

As you work through this module, keep in mind that vital information also includes important personal documents that need to be stored in a safe location such as insurance policies, deeds, and property records. Ideally they should be kept in a safety deposit box away from your home. However, you need to make copies of important documents to keep in your emergency supply kit (See *Module 3: If We Need to Evacuate* on building and emergency supply kit). It is also wise to make a record of your personal property, for insurance purposes. Take photos or a video of the interior and exterior of your home and include personal belongings in your inventory.

And one other item of vital interest is money. Consider saving money in an emergency savings account that could be used in any crisis. It is advisable to keep a small amount of cash or traveler's checks at home in a safe place where you can quickly access them in case of evacuation.

Addressing the area of Vital Information involves many elements common to all families, however, it is important for your family to gather together and discuss those issues that are specific to you. This is especially vital in the area of elderly or disabled family members or those with special medical needs that require immediate attention. Time invested in developing your family's Vital Information is a critical step in emergency preparedness, but it is no less critical than reviewing that information and updating it frequently.

Worksheet and Supplemental Materials
Fill out *Worksheet: Vital Information Card*
Download the Vital Information Card wallet templates:
http://www.ready.gov/sites/default/files/documents/files/Family_Emegency_Plan.pdf

Module 6:
Home Escape Plan Tool

Did you know?

- A small flame can get out of control and turn into a large, uncontrollable fire in less than 30 seconds.

- Only 26 percent of families have actually developed and practiced a home fire escape plan.

- Eighty percent of Americans don't realize that home fires are the single most common disaster across the nation.

- The number of home fires the American Red Cross has responded to has risen 10% since 2000.

- Every two and a half hours someone is killed in a home fire. In a typical year, 20,000 people are injured in home fires.

- Having a working smoke alarm reduces one's chances of dying in a fire by nearly half.

- Children and older adults are twice as likely to die in a home fire as the American population at large.

And yet, fire is one emergency that we can do a lot to prepare for. In this module we will discuss some preparedness tips and show you how to develop your own family escape route.

Preparedness Tips

Here are some general tips for you to consider incorporating into to your emergency planning.

- Install a smoke alarm on every level of your home and outside of sleeping areas. Install a carbon monoxide alarm on each level of your home.

- Test smoke alarm batteries every month and change them at least once a year.

- Make sure everyone in your family knows at least two ways to escape from every room of your home.

- Practice your fire escape plan at least twice a year. Designate a meeting spot outside and a safe distance from your home. Make sure all family members know the meeting spot.

- Have your family practice escaping from your home, practicing low crawling and at different times of the day. Make sure everyone knows how to call 9-1-1.

- Consider escape ladders for sleeping areas on the second or third floor. Make sure everyone in your home learns how to use them ahead of time by reading the manufacturer's instructions and understanding the steps to use them. Store them near the window where they will be used.

Planning Your Family Escape Route

- Plan for at least two ways to escape from each room.

- If you live in a multi-story apartment building, map out as many routes of escape as possible to exit stairways on your floor of the building.

- If you live in a high-rise, plan to use the stairs, never the elevator, to escape a fire.

- A secondary route might be a window onto an adjacent roof or a collapsible ladder for escape from upper-story windows. Purchase only collapsible ladders evaluated by a nationally recognized laboratory, such as Underwriters Laboratory (UL).

- Develop a plan for everyone in your home, including babies and others who need help to escape.

- Pick a meeting location away from your home.

- Practice your escape plan every month and practice from every room.

- Practice getting out with your eyes closed, crawling low to the floor, and keeping your mouth covered.

- Involve children in making and practicing your escape plan and teach them to never hide during a fire; they must get out and stay out.

- Clear toys, boxes and other debris from exits and check that windows open easily; immediately fixing any that stick.

- Be sure that security bars on doors and windows have a quick-release latch, and everyone knows how to open them.

In this next section we have provided a grid to draw a diagram of your home. Make a diagram of every floor and don't forget the basement. Be sure to mark all windows and doors. Then sit down with your family and plan two exits from every room. Be sure that your children have a hand in determining the escape route from their bedroom.

Worksheet and Supplemental Materials
Fill out *Worksheet: Home Escape Plan Tool*

Help us spread Reverse 911 in your community.

Please share the free PDF version of this book or order additional copies as gifts for your friends, neighbors and coworkers through our web site:

To share with friends: http://safetyinformed.org/share

You can support us by ordering copies of this book through Amazon.com: http://safetyinformed.org/order/epw

Share Reverse 911 with Family, Friends, Neighbors and Co-Workers

Help us spread Reverse 911 in your community. *Less than 10% of the U.S. population has registered a mobile device with a local Reverse 911 alert system.* This serious shortfall reduces the effectiveness of Emergency Notification Systems. Our goal is to educate as many people as possible about Reverse 911, as most people think that the wireless alerts they automatically receive on their cell phones are adequate. Those alerts are from Federal authorities and often refer you to local news. Not effective as the precise warnings and instructions they would receive from local fire, police, and emergency authorities through Reverse 911!

Please help us spread the word about registering mobile devices with Reverse 911 through your family, friends, neighbors, and co-workers by sharing our free resources. We've made it easy and will only take a few seconds. Visit the page below select where you'd like to share!

http://safetyinformed.org/share

Did you find our service useful?

Please consider a small donation to fund our efforts. Our staff is small so any donation goes a long way toward our goal of reaching the millions of mobile device users nationwide.

http://safetyinformed.org/donate

SafetyInformed operates under the fiscal sponsorship of Social Good Fund, a tax-exempt 501c(3) charitable organization. All donations are tax deductable.

You can also support us by ordering copies of this book through Amazon.com: http://safetyinformed.org/order/epw

Follow Us:

If you haven't already, follow us on one of your favorite social media sites below or visit our blog to receive useful tips on Emergency Planning and Home Safety.

Blog: http://SafetyInformed.com/blog
Facebook: http://facebook.com/safetyinformed
Twitter: http://twitter.com/safetyinformed
Google+: http://google.com/+SafetyinformedUniversity

SafetyInformed.org's

Emergency Plan

Worksheets

Worksheet: Family Emergency Plan

Family Name _____

Address _____

Date Updated _____

A Family Emergency Plan is one of the most important steps you can take to prepare for a disaster at your home, your neighborhood or in your region. Safety is a matter of awareness, knowledge and preparation. Your plan can prepare your family members to make good decisions in an emergency.

Disasters can strike quickly and without warning and can force you to evacuate your neighborhood or confine you to your home. What would you do if basic services--water, gas, electricity or telephones--were cut off? Local officials and relief workers will be on the scene after a disaster, but they cannot reach everyone right away. Families must prepare for an emergency in advance so that they understand what they must do and where they must go if and when an emergency arises. Discuss the plan with everyone involved and practice sheltering at home, evacuation escape routes and going to meeting places. Have copies of the Plan stored where they will be readily available when needed. Update the plan whenever situations change or at least annually.

What are the type of emergencies and hazards in my area?

Discuss the types of emergencies that are possible in your area. Good examples can be found in our *Disaster Preparedness Library* at:

> http://safetyinformed.org/education/hazard

What should each member of your family do in each situation?

This plan template and is intended to give you a format and possible suggestions about information you might want to include in a family emergency plan. It is not all-inclusive and should be modified by the user to suit individual or family needs.

Additional Steps to Consider:

- Store emergency supplies to meet your possible needs for three days after an emergency

- Compile and securely store vital documents and records

- Compile a medical and medication history for each family member

- Learn basic First Aid and CPR

Before you can prepare, you must determine what you are preparing to survive and how each disaster threatens you, your safety and survival. But first, it's important to realize that you cannot prepare for everything. So it's critical to meet with household members. Discuss with children the dangers of fire, severe weather, earthquakes, industrial accidents and other emergencies and how you need to respond to each one.

There are a lot of basic things to make sure the whole family is aware of, such as:

- What to do about power outages and personal injuries.

- Make a floor plan of your home and mark all escape routes from each room.

- Everyone should know how to turn off the water, gas, and electricity at main switches.

- You need a good communication plan with all emergency telephone numbers near telephones. Children should be taught how and when to call 911, police, and fire.

- Have emergency radios available and note where to tune for emergency information.

- Establish one out-of-state and one local friend or relative for family members to call if separated by disaster.

These are just some examples of the things you need to consider in developing your Basic Emergency Plan.

In the following sections we will help you get started building your plan and the first place to start is making sure you are registered with local Reverse 911 system so you won't miss important alerts for community emergencies, natural disasters, industrial accidents, evacuation orders, shelter-in-place, and severe weather events.

How will we know danger is near?

_____ Set up Reverse 911 alerts for all areas of concern.

SafetyInformed's easy to use ZIP code search will find Reverse 911 alerts for your area within seconds. Login via the link below and then click "Search" on the top menu. If you haven't set up an account there, it's free.

Here's the link to login or signup for a new account: http://*safetyinformed.org/*myaccount

_____ TV station   _____Radio stations No.

_____ We have a battery powered or hand crank radio?

_____ Other:

Where will we take shelter inside our home in case of an emergency?

_____

_____

(Select an interior room, structurally secure, without windows. Supplies to keep in this space: first aid kit, flashlight, radio).

Where will we assemble if we cannot assemble at home or in our area?

(This should be a location in a different city or area from where your home is located. The location should be very familiar to your family such as a friend/family member's home, place of business, public landmark or church).

Name of Location/Person:

Address:

Phone Numbers: 1.   2.   3.

Brief Directions:

Notes:

What is our immediate plan of action to assemble if communications are down?

If a disaster or emergency occurs while we are away from home, who will do what? (i.e. Mom picks up Jennifer from school, Dad picks of Danny from daycare and then grandma).

Person Responsible	Responsible For: Person and their special needs *(meds, medical equipment, etc.)*

Is there anything else that will need to be done?

(Gather pets and their supplies, move livestock, check on neighbors, etc.)

Person Responsible	Responsible For

School and Day Care Emergency Response Plans:

(Ask for copies of their plans)

School	Evacuation Site Address and Phone

Worksheet:
If We Have To Evacuate

In some cases when you need to evacuate, there may not be a lot of time. Therefore it's important that everyone know at least two ways to exit your house. You need to make sure that everyone is able to reach the ground using a walk out, ladder, rope, roof, etc. The key is for everyone to know your family evacuation-plan and how it ties into your overall disaster plan.

There are many other things to consider, not the least of which is to determine whether or not you need to evacuate. That's where preplanning is so important, in an emergency there is often not enough time to discuss your options. In this section we look at preparing for the time when you need to evacuate.

In many emergencies we should shelter at home both during and after the event. Sometimes we will need to evacuate either to a location close by or farther away.

Who is evacuating with us?

1.

2.

3.

4.

5.

Escape routes from our home:

Escape routes from our home:

What do we need to do before leaving home?

Person Responsible	Task Responsible For
	Collect Go Bags for each person including prescription meds and a copy of this plan
	Vital records, lap top PCs or backup files
	Turn off utilities
	Contact someone outside the area with our plans
	Leave a note for First Responders with our name, where we are going and contact info

What form of transportation will we use?

1.

2.

3.

Alternate route #1:   *Alternate route #2:*

_____   _____

_____   _____

_____   _____

_____   _____

What vital items/ records do we need to take with us?

Person Responsible	Item/Document

What keepsakes do we need to take with us?

Person Responsible	Item

Pet Information

Where can we leave our pets if we evacuate?

Family Name:

Address:

Phone:

Name	Breed	Age

List any other information about your pets

(i.e. license information, immunizations, prescriptions, special instructions, medical information) as well as a link to a current photo of your pet online. *(Current photos are extremely important for identifying your pet if it were to become separated from your family).*

	Name	**Name**
License Information		
Immunizations		
Prescriptions		
Special Instructions		
Medical Information		
Other		

Notes:

Local Evacuation Location

If we have to evacuate our home, but the immediate area is still safe, where will we live temporarily?

Name of Location/Person:

Address:

Phone Numbers: 1.   2.   3.

Brief Directions:

Notes:

Regional Evacuation Location

If we have to evacuate our home and the immediate area/city, where will we live temporarily?

Name of Location/Person:

Address:

Phone Numbers: 1.   2.   3.

Brief Directions:

Notes:

Out of State Evacuation Location

If we have to evacuate our home and the state/region where will we live temporarily?

Name of Location/Person:

Address:

Phone Numbers: 1.   2.   3.

Brief Directions:

Notes:

Worksheet:
Emergency Communication Plan

There are three main purposes to consider when communicating with someone as part of your *Emergency Communication Plan*:

1. To order the initiation or change to a part of your emergency plan.

2. To acknowledge or communicate that a certain part has begun or changed.

3. To pass on information as to your status or requirements—as the situation dictates.

Your communication plan should be an intimate part of your over all emergency plan, whether that plan is to remain in your home or exit to a pre-planned or agreed upon location. If you're just planning for how to communicate with your family in case of something like a fire or car accident or something, your communication plan will vary somewhat. But in all cases if your plan is to be effective it has to be Clear, Complete, Concise, and Confirmed. You need to ensure that they get the whole story. Once you've figured out how to get your message across clearly, you need to make sure it's as concise as possible. Communications in emergency situations is sometimes iffy and people have other things on their mind such as getting out of danger or performing first aid.

In this section we take a look at establishing a good family communication plan by asking the question, how do we plan to communicate during/after a disaster or emergency?

List the top three ways you plan to communicate so that everyone is communicating in the same way.

Remember cell phones may not be working and phone lines may be busy Text messages sometimes go through when voice calls do not. You might want to agree to meet at a specific location or to contact a specified family member or friend.

1.

2.

3.

Who is the main point of contact in our immediate family?

List two people who should be the point person for all contact. This will eliminate conflicting messages and confusion if everyone is making contact with only two people.)

1.

2.

Who is our main point of contact in our extended family, friends or neighbors?

List two people who will be a point of contact for updates on the family's location and status of well-being. These should be people who are naturally concerned for your well-being and whom you can trust to inform others of your situation when needed.

Name	Cell Phone	Home phone	Work Phone	Email

Immediate family member's contact information:

	Name	Name	Name	Name
Email Address				
Phone-work and cell				
Facebook				
Twitter				
Link to Current Picture				

Professional Contacts:

(List doctors, insurance agents, attorney, CPA, any professional you may need to contact).

Name	Address	Phone Number

Other Important Contacts:

(List people from work, school, church, clubs, etc.)

Name	Address	Phone Number

Contact extended family, friends and neighbors contact information:

Name	Address	Phone Number

Notes:

First Responder Phone Numbers:

Emergencies 411, Non Emergencies 311

Police Department: _____

Fire   Department:_____

FEMA: (202) 566-1600

Red Cross: (800) 733-2767

National Weather: (301) 713-4000

Worksheet: Vital Information Card

Start by discussing with your family the contact information you'll need to fill out your individual Vital Information Cards with the form below:

NAME _____

ADDRESS _____

_____

Out of Town Contact (Address/Phone) _____

_____

Health Conditions _____

Medications/Dosages _____

Family Dr. Name/Phone _____

Parent/Caregiver Name _____

Relationship_____

Home Phone_____

Work Phone_____

Cell Phone_____

Emergency Contact Name/Address

_____

_____

_____

Phone Number _____

Out of Town Contact Name/Address

_____

_____

_____

Phone Number _____

Neighborhood Meeting Place

_____

_____

_____

Phone Number _____

Other Important Information:

Now download the wallet card template at the link below and transfer the appropriate information to each family member's wallet card:

http://www.ready.gov/sites/default/files/documents/files/Family_Emegency_Plan.pdf

ADDITIONAL IMPORTANT PHONE NUMBERS & INFORMATION:

Family Emergency Plan

EMERGENCY CONTACT NAME:
TELEPHONE:

OUT-OF-TOWN CONTACT NAME:
TELEPHONE:

NEIGHBORHOOD MEETING PLACE:
TELEPHONE:

OTHER IMPORTANT INFORMATION:

Ready

DIAL 911 FOR EMERGENCIES

Worksheet: Home Escape Tool

Here are six key steps to follow in creating your family's escape plan.

Step 1: As a family draw a floor plan of your home. Include all window and doors. Use your own graph paper or download a free printable version through: http://www.printfreegraphpaper.com

Use a page for each level in your home.

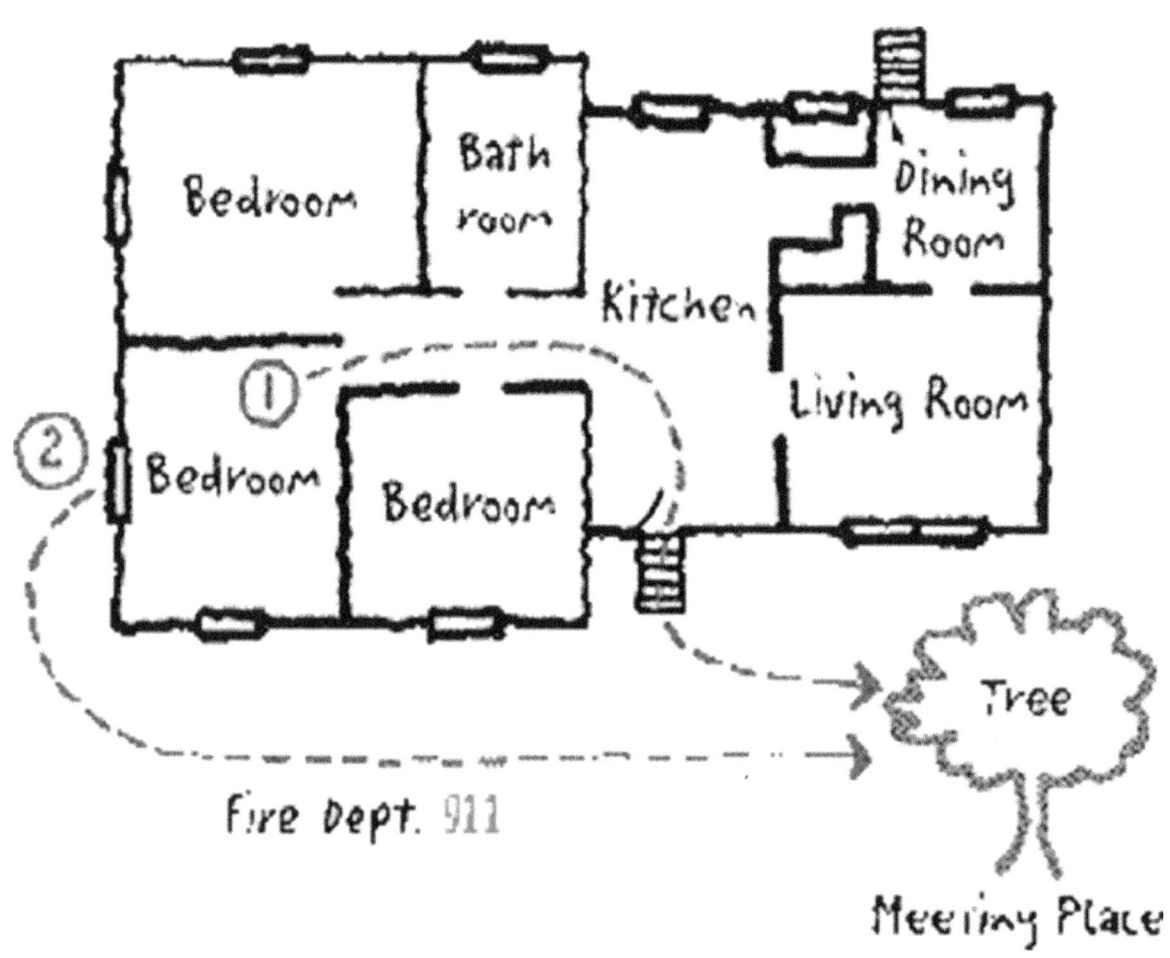

Step 2: Show two ways out of each room, in case your main route is blocked by smoke or flame. Make sure windows can be opened easily.

Step 3: Pick an outside meeting place for all family members to meet and wait for the fire department or first responders.

Step 4: Install smoke alarms near every sleeping area and on each level of your home. Install Carbon Monoxide alarms on each level of your home.

Step 5: Practice your evacuation plan at least twice a year. Make sure all children understand the escape plan.

Step 6: Once out, stay out! Don't go back inside for any reason. Make sure children understand not to go back into the house to look for their parents. Stay at the meeting place.

Notes: